JOHN LESLEY
CONTINENTS OF THE WORLD
Australia
REDBACK publishing

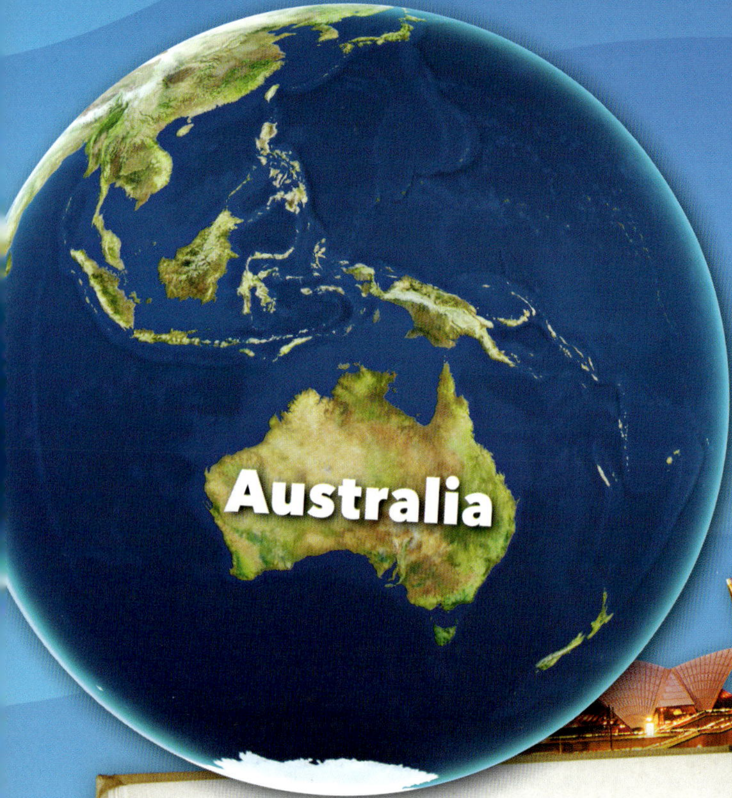

Australia

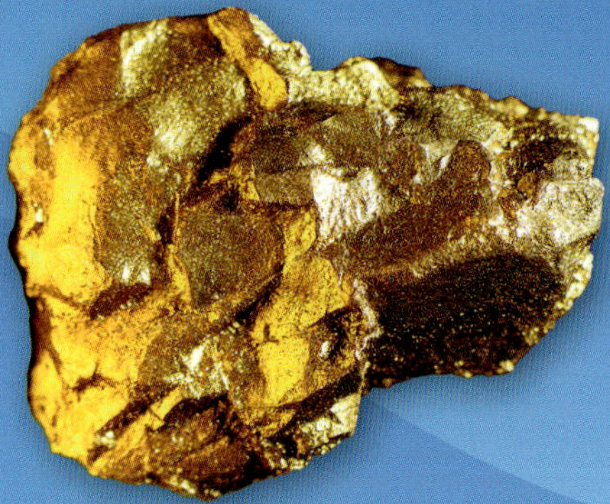

Wealth from the Earth p.26

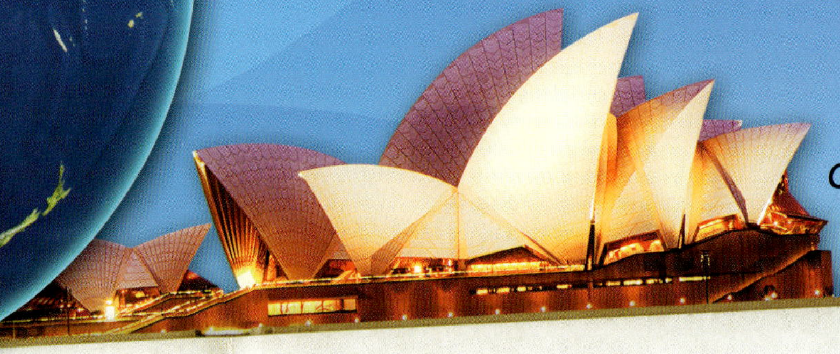

Cities p.18

Redback Publishing
Suite 6, 13a Narabang Way,
Belrose NSW 2085
Australia

www.redbackpublishing.com
orders@redbackpublishing.com

ISBN 978-1-761400-97-1

Author: John Lesley
Editor: Caroline Thomas
Designer: Redback Publishing

Originated by Redback Publishing

Acknowledgements
Abbreviations: l—left, r—right, b—bottom, t—top, c—centre, m—middle

We would like to thank the following for permission to reproduce photographs (images © Shutterstock unless otherwise stated): p2tl, p19mr Sydney, Australia, Taras Vyshnya, p3mr, p12br typical Papuan boats, Anna_plucinska, p10tr Great Dividing Range map, Ordinary Person, CC BY-SA 4.0 (https://creativecommons.org/licenses/by-sa/4.0), via Wikimedia Commons, p10bc Uluru, Benny Marty, p13br The 1893 Brisbane flood, Public domain, via Wikimedia Commons, p17tr New Guinea, Indonesia, Sergey Uryadnikov, p18bl Port of Sorong, Hardscarf, via Wikipedia Commons, p18br Jayapura, Papua, Indonesia, Wika Papua, p20tl Baliem Valley Festival, Wamena, Papua New Guinea, Indonesia, Tanya Keisha, p20bl Adelaide, myphotobank.com.au, p21tr St Mary's Cathedral, Sydney, byvalet, p21ml church service, Palembe, Papua New Guinea, Michal Knitl, p22bl Aboriginal artists, ChameleonsEye, p23mr Pioneer settlers from The Powerhouse Museum Collection, Public domain, via Wikimedia Commons, p26ml Mary Kathleen uranium mine, Queensland, Geomartin, CC BY 3.0 (https://creativecommons.org/licenses/by/3.0), via Wikimedia Commons, p26bc Ok Tedi Mine, Papua New Guinea, Ok Tedi Mine CMCA Review, via Wikimedia Commons, p30br Sydney, Australia, marcobrivio.photo, p30c Uluru, bmphotographer

A catalogue record for this book is available from the National Library of Australia

Contents

Mighty Rivers p.12

Wildlife p.24

People and Religions p.20

Earth's 7 Continents

What is a continent?

A continent is a very large landmass which is separated from others on Earth. Some are separated by oceans, but others have land borders with each other.

Or are there 5?

Some people group Europe and Asia into one continent called Eurasia, and they combine North and South America into the Americas. According to this method of counting, there are five continents instead of seven.

Origin of Australia

How did the continents form?

The surface of our planet is constantly moving in a very slow process known as plate tectonics. The plates are gigantic slabs of rock that form the surface of our Earth. These plates rest on magma that is hotter and more liquid as it gets deeper towards the Earth's centre. As the heat rises out towards the surface of the Earth, it causes the plates to move around.

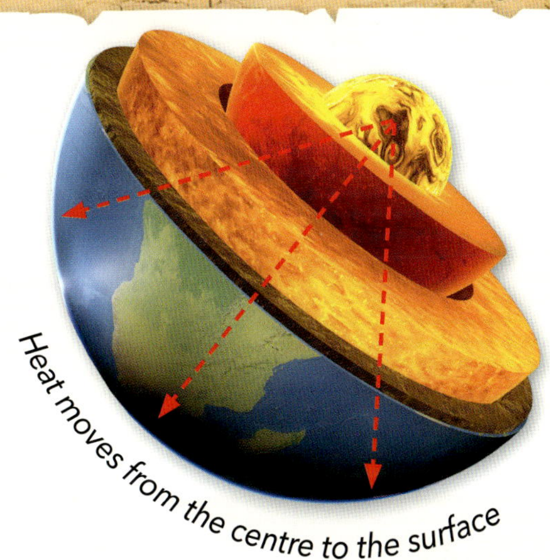

Heat moves from the centre to the surface

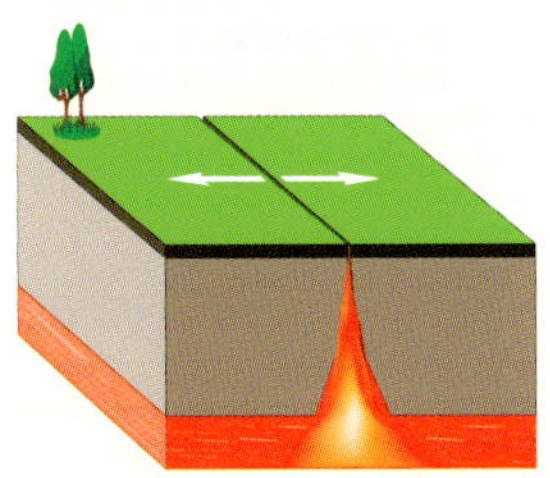

Plates pull apart

Plates push together

When these plates move, their edges can either pull apart or push together. Where the plates pull apart, oceans can flow between the landmasses, and where they push together, mountain ranges can form. This process explains how continents form over very long periods of time.

Gondwana

The continents have not always been in the same location as they are now. Millions of years ago, they were parts of other huge masses of land. We call one of these Gondwana, and it was that piece of land that eventually became Australia and New Guinea.

The Continent of Australia

The Australian Continent

The continent of Australia is not the same as the nation of Australia, which is only a part of the whole continent.

The other parts of the continent include the island of New Guinea, as well as a number of smaller islands and the island state of Tasmania.

All of these places are on the same tectonic plate, and together they are moving slowly northwards across the Earth's surface at a rate of a few centimetres each year.

View from the southeast Australian coastline of the Tasman Sea

Seas

The seas surrounding the Australian continent are:

Arafura Sea – north of Australia, separating it from New Guinea

Bismarck Sea – north of Papua New Guinea

Coral Sea – northeast of Australia, separating it from Papua New Guinea and the Solomon Islands

Tasman Sea – between Australia and New Zealand

Timor Sea – between northwest Australia and Timor

Australia covers about 5% of the world's landmass.

Sealife at the Great Barrier Reef in the Coral Sea

Oceans

The oceans surrounding Australia are:

Pacific Ocean - east of Australia and north of New Guinea

Indian Ocean - west of Australia

Southern Ocean - between Australia and Antarctica

New Zealand and the islands in the Pacific Ocean near Australia are usually included in a region called Oceania.

"Girt By Sea"

The Australian national anthem includes the words "girt by sea". This phrase refers to the oceans that surround the country of Australia.

Continental Shelf

During the last Ice Age, which ended about 10,000 years ago, the world's sea levels were lower than they are now. At that time, some of Australia's continental shelves were dry land, making the continent much bigger than it is today.

Where a continent is bounded by an ocean, the land at the ocean's edge often continues under the water as a continental shelf. This shelf may end abruptly at a point where the underwater rocks drop down to a deep ocean abyss.

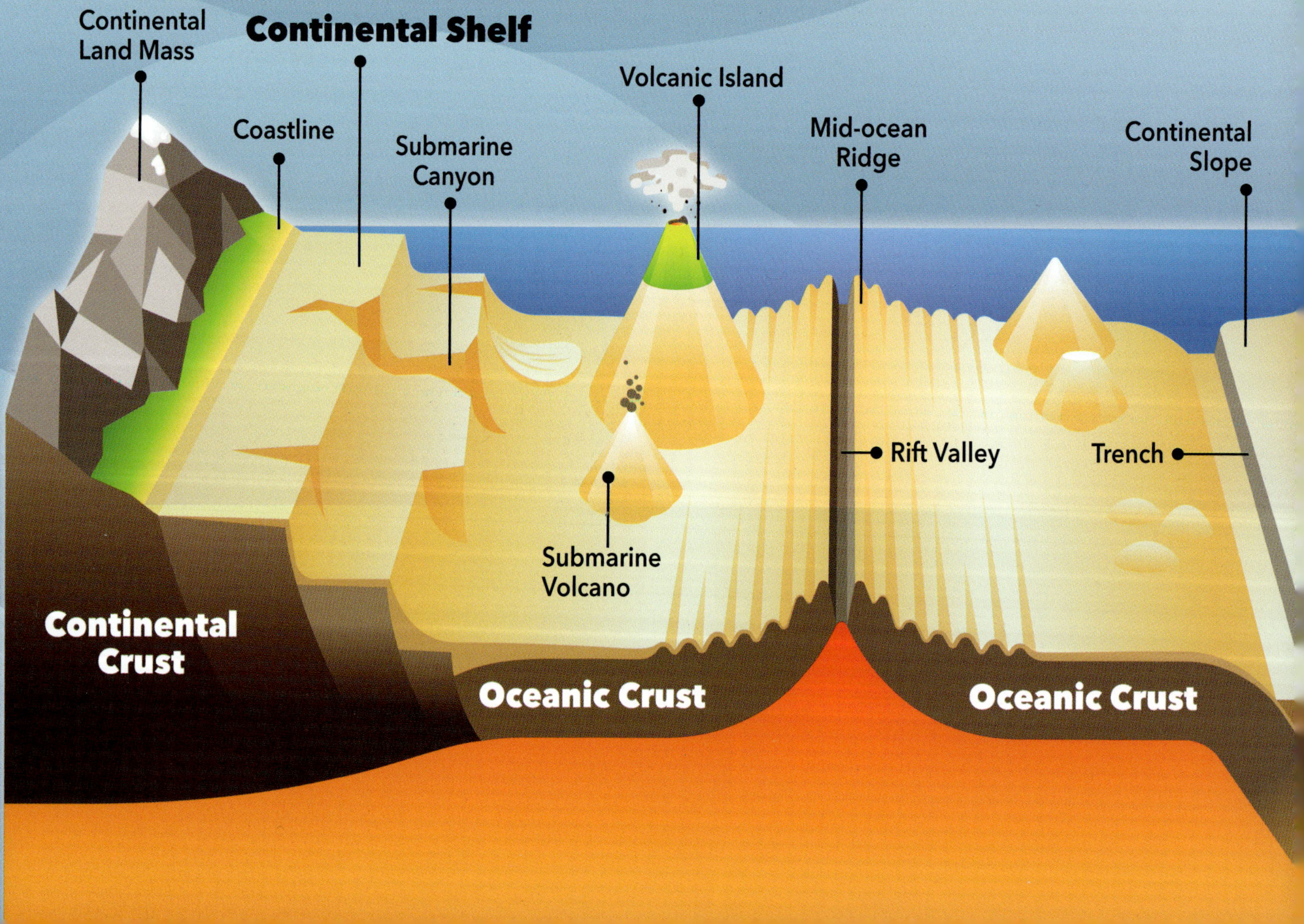

Continental Land Mass

Continental Shelf

Coastline

Submarine Canyon

Volcanic Island

Mid-ocean Ridge

Continental Slope

Rift Valley

Trench

Submarine Volcano

Continental Crust

Oceanic Crust

Oceanic Crust

At an ocean boundary, each country can claim control over the ocean and the continental shelf for a distance of 200 nautical miles from the shore. This distance is set by member countries of the United Nations under the UNCLOS agreement.

The Great Barrier Reef

The Great Barrier Reef, off the east coast of Queensland, sits on Australia's continental shelf. Thousands of years ago, this area was dry land, and the Indigenous people living there could walk across it.

UNCLOS

The United Nations Convention on the Law of the Sea (UNCLOS) sets rules that countries use to determine who has control over the water and the seafloor at a nation's ocean boundary.

Tasmania

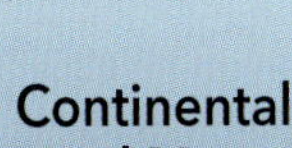

Tasmania

Tasmania and the mainland of Australia were once joined by dry land. The continental shelf between them is now covered by the waters of Bass Strait, but it was dry land only about 10,000 years ago. Up until then, Indigenous people migrated to Tasmania, where they settled across the whole island. These people were isolated in Tasmania when sea levels rose as the Earth's climate began warming.

The Island of New Guinea

The mainland of Australia was also once joined to the island of New Guinea by very shallow seas dotted with small islands. People from both sides could have easily travelled between the two lands.

The Land

The Nation of Australia

The Great Diving Range

The Great Dividing Range is a long range of mountains that stretches all the way down the east of Australia. It even extends under the sea into Tasmania.

On the mainland of Australia, this mountain range blocks moisture-laden air from reaching the inland. It is largely responsible for the vast difference in climate and landscapes between the temperate and sub-tropical east coast, and the semi-arid inland.

Ancient River

The Finke River in central Australia is one of the oldest existing rivers anywhere on our planet. It has been flowing along a similar course for millions of years.

Ancient Rocks

The central desert regions of Australia have some of the oldest rocks on Earth. They date from three and a half billion years ago. Our planet is four and a half billion years old, so Australia's ancient rocks date from the early part of Earth's existence.

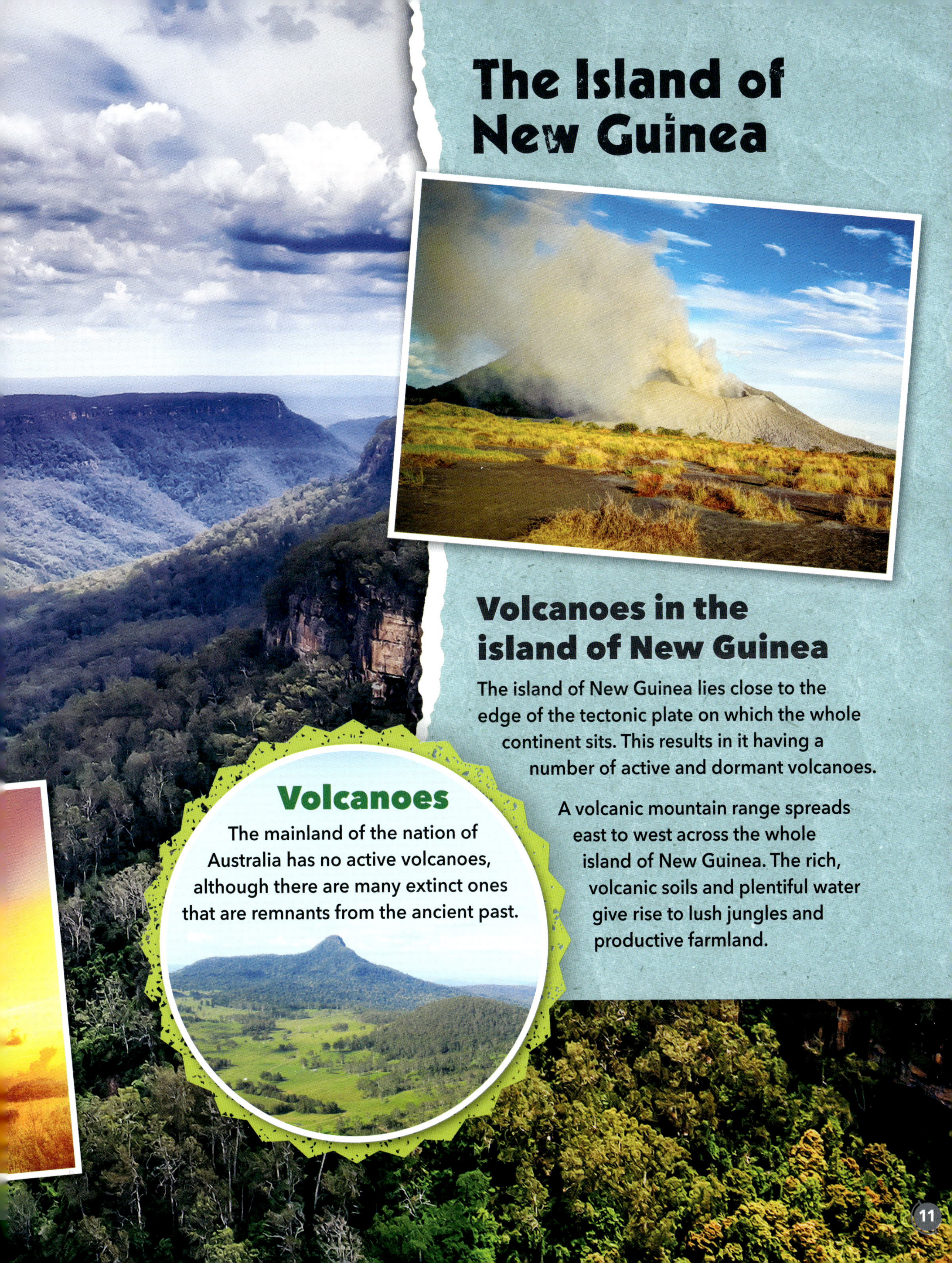

The Island of New Guinea

Volcanoes in the island of New Guinea

The island of New Guinea lies close to the edge of the tectonic plate on which the whole continent sits. This results in it having a number of active and dormant volcanoes.

A volcanic mountain range spreads east to west across the whole island of New Guinea. The rich, volcanic soils and plentiful water give rise to lush jungles and productive farmland.

Volcanoes

The mainland of the nation of Australia has no active volcanoes, although there are many extinct ones that are remnants from the ancient past.

Mighty Rivers

Murray-Darling River (Australia)

Australia's longest river system is the Murray-Darling River. Millions of people depend on the river, and its waters are vital for agriculture in the farmland through which it flows.

The Murray Darling River system rises in Queensland, continues on through New South Wales and Victoria, and enters the sea at Goolwa in South Australia.

Sepik River (New Guinea)

The Sepik River is one of the longest rivers in all of New Guinea. It flows past dense jungles, open farmland and through wetlands or swamps. There are no large dams in this mighty river, and irrigation channels are not needed for agriculture because of the high rainfall in New Guinea.

The richness of its natural and cultural diversity has earned the Upper Sepik River Basin a place on UNESCO's tentative list for future World Heritage listing.

Papuan residents prepare traditional canoes at the Pagwi township on the Sepik River in Papua New Guinea.

Droughts and Floods

The nation of Australia is prone to regular cycles of drought and flooding

Tough Enough

During droughts, farmers need to use underground, artesian water sources. Farmers choose crops and livestock that are hardy enough to withstand times when there is a reduced water supply.

Monsoonal Rainfall

The periodical flooding of rivers across the inland regions is often a result of monsoonal rainfall in the north. Riverbeds that have been dry for long periods quickly fill as water flows downstream.

The 2019 Townsville flood

High Ground

The first British settlers in Australia endured massive destruction of their early settlements through flooding in the early 1800s. This prompted governments to order that new towns had to be positioned on high ground rather than right next to local rivers.

The 1893 Brisbane flood

Highest and Lowest Places

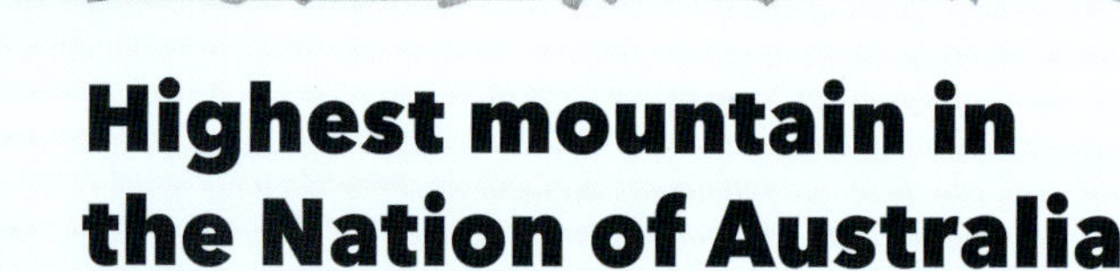

Highest mountain in the Nation of Australia

Mount Kosciuszko, New South Wales, at 2,228 metres high

Lowest location in the Nation of Australia

Kati Thanda-Lake Eyre, South Australia, 15 metres below sea level.

This salt lake remains dry for long periods and then suddenly fills with water after heavy rains to the north. Wildlife somehow knows when this is happening, and all sorts of animals, from tiny to large, converge on the lake from long distances away.

Highest mountains in the Island of New Guinea

Puncak Jaya, in Indonesian Papua, 4,884 metres high

Mount Wilhelm, in Papua New Guinea, 4,509 metres high

Climate of Australia

The Nation of Australia

The climate across the nation of Australia ranges from hot and tropical in the north, to dry and hot in the centre and the Outback. Northern Australia has a wet and dry season, with heavy rains and strong winds brought by the annual monsoon. Southern parts of Australia have four seasons, although traditional, Indigenous knowledge divides the year into more seasonal periods, each with very detailed descriptions.

In the mountains of Tasmania and the Southern Alps on the mainland, the climate is alpine, with snow falling during the winter.

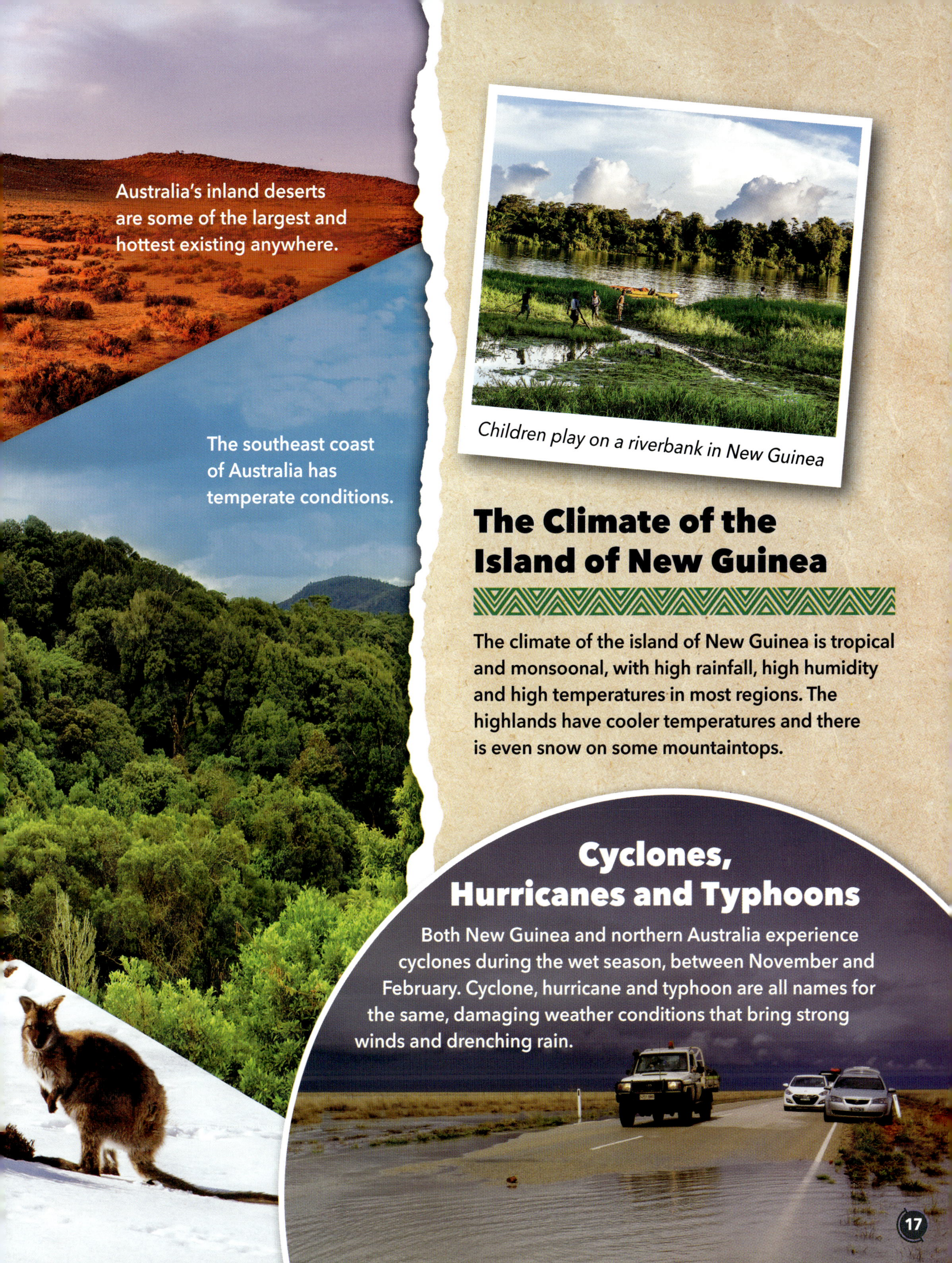

Australia's inland deserts are some of the largest and hottest existing anywhere.

The southeast coast of Australia has temperate conditions.

Children play on a riverbank in New Guinea

The Climate of the Island of New Guinea

The climate of the island of New Guinea is tropical and monsoonal, with high rainfall, high humidity and high temperatures in most regions. The highlands have cooler temperatures and there is even snow on some mountaintops.

Cyclones, Hurricanes and Typhoons

Both New Guinea and northern Australia experience cyclones during the wet season, between November and February. Cyclone, hurricane and typhoon are all names for the same, damaging weather conditions that bring strong winds and drenching rain.

Cities on the Australian Continent

Canberra

Sorong

Indonesian Provinces

- **Papua** is the most easterly province of Indonesia. Its capital city is **Jayapura**.
- **West Papua**, which is located on the west coast of the island of New Guinea, is also a province of Indonesia. Its largest city is **Sorong**.

Melbourne

Canberra
Sydney
Melbourne

The Nation of Australia

Capital city - **Canberra**

Largest cities - **Sydney** and **Melbourne**

Sydney

Papua New Guinea

Capital city - **Port Moresby**

Papua, Indonesia
Papua New Guinea
Port Moresby

People and Religions

Population of the Island of New Guinea

Papua New Guinea has about 9 million people. The Indonesian provinces of West Papua and Papua have about 4 million people.

The majority of New Guinea's people live in traditional villages, but there are also cities with modern educational, medical and social facilities.

There are hundreds of different indigenous languages spoken throughout New Guinea.

Population of the Nation of Australia

The nation of Australia has a population of 26 million, of whom about 3% are Indigenous people.

Australian people come from a range of ethnicities. Immigrants from Britain were the most numerous for many years, but people from hundreds of other countries now also make Australia their home.

The people in the nation of Australia are some of the most urbanised anywhere. About 90% of them live in cities and towns.

Religions in the Nation of Australia

Because of Australia's immigration history, Christianity has become the main religion, with Islam, Buddhism and Hinduism having the next largest numbers of followers. There is also a very large group of people who claim to have no religious beliefs at all.

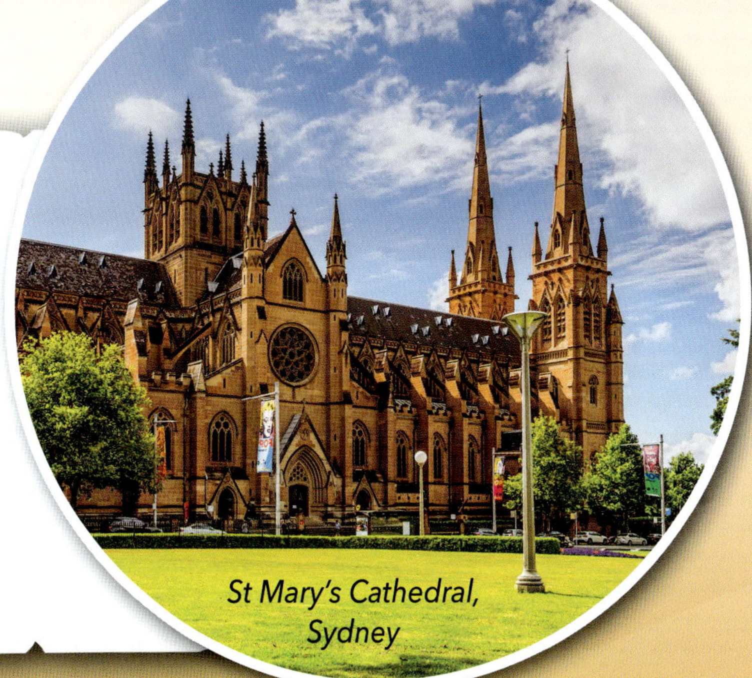

St Mary's Cathedral, Sydney

Religions in the Island of New Guinea

Christianity is a leading religion across Papua New Guinea, as a result of decades of visits by Christian missionaries. Most of the indigenous people, including many who are Christians, also follow traditional religious beliefs and customs. In Indonesian New Guinea, Islam is the most popular religion.

Spirit Houses

Papua New Guinea's 'spirit houses', with their high, pointed roofs, are traditional religious places found in many villages. They are often covered in elaborate carvings and decoration.

Landscapes and Culture

Across the continent of Australia, the different types of landscapes have affected the way human societies and their cultures developed.

Indigenous Peoples

Australia's Indigenous peoples have been living on the land for over 60,000 years. They lived on the coasts, in the deserts, on small islands, beside rivers and in cool, mountainous regions. Their lifestyles, food sources and creative cultures all developed differently depending on the surroundings.

Aboriginal artists create a dot painting

Indigenous people living in cool climates developed the art of making decorated, fur cloaks, and those in the central desert regions created the widely admired dot painting style of art.

Recent Migration

People from many countries have migrated to Australia in large numbers since the end of the Second World War in 1945. They have mostly settled in coastal cities or large towns inland, where there are good opportunities for employment and education.

European Settlers

European settlers began arriving in 1788. At first they lived in towns on the coasts, where there was a supply of fresh water from rivers that did not dry up.

Farmers later moved to the plains and grasslands further inland, where they often had to dig deep wells to draw water for themselves and their livestock.

The Island of New Guinea

New Guinea is a mountainous island. The majority of the population farm their own land and live in villages. **Subsistence farming** is common, because there are no vast plains or grasslands where agricultural crops or large herds of livestock can be farmed.

Wildlife Wonders

Marsupials

The islands of Australia and New Guinea are both home to the largest diversity of marsupial mammals on Earth. The Australian kangaroo and koala are two well-known examples, but there are also wombats, Tasmanian devils, possums, wallabies and many more. New Guinea's own marsupials include tree kangaroos and the cuscus.

Tree kangaroo

Platypus

Monotremes

Although marsupials are the most famous of the continent's wildlife, there is also another animal group that is unique and fascinating. These are the monotremes, and they include the platypus and echidna. These surprising creatures are mammals and have fur, but they also lay eggs and feed their babies on milk from the mother's body.

Echidna

How are marsupials different?

Marsupials give birth to very underdeveloped young. These tiny offspring climb into the mother's pouch and continue to grow there until they are big enough to leave and live by themselves.

Kangaroo and joey

Ringtail possum

Why are these animals only on the Australian Continent?

The islands of Australia and New Guinea were once joined, so their wildlife could travel freely back and forth. When the sea levels rose thousands of years ago, the animals on each of the islands continued to evolve in isolation from the rest of the world.

Placentals

Placental mammals give birth to live babies that have grown inside the mother. Dingoes are placental mammals, not marsupials or monotremes. They are Australia's own native dog and have probably only been in the country for a few thousand years.

A relative of the dingo still exists in remote parts of New Guinea, suggesting that people may have brought the ancestors of the Australian dingo with them when they travelled to the island of Australia in prehistoric times.

Wealth from the Earth

The continent of Australia is rich in mineral resources, including the ores of iron, aluminium, copper, nickel, zinc and lead. There are also areas both onshore and offshore that have oil and natural gas reserves.

Uranium

The nation of Australia has vast amounts of uranium ore in the ground. Uranium is used in other countries to produce electricity and for nuclear weapons.

Mary Kathleen, a former uranium mine, Queensland

Mining in New Guinea

Mining contributes significantly to New Guinea's economy. Mining for cobalt, copper, gold, nickel and silver, as well as for oil and natural gas, are important sources of income and employment for the island.

Iron Ore

The nation of Australia mines and exports large quantities of iron ore.

Coal

Coal mines across the nation of Australia produce coal that is used for electricity production both locally and in other countries around the world.

Ok Tedi Mine, Papua New Guinea

The Environment

Australians are very conscious of the importance of preserving their unique wildlife and precious natural wildernesses.

Great Barrier Reef

This coral reef is one of the largest in the world. It is threatened by the warming of ocean waters, which causes corals to lose their colour and then die. The invasive Crown of Thorns starfish has been a reef pest for many years. The flow of silt and chemicals in rivers that empty onto the reef has the potential to damage the delicate coral.

Wildlife

The main threat to Australia's wildlife comes from the reduction in their natural habitats due to the increase in human population and the landscape changes this produces.

Rainforests

Rainforests are threatened by global warming, as high temperatures and changes in rainfall increase the risk of fire and drying of the environment. Fortunately, World Heritage listed rainforests are protected from logging, or clearing for farmland and housing developments.

Desert Wildernesses

Australia's enormous deserts are some of the harshest places on Earth, yet they support a diverse range of life including reptiles, birds, marsupials and rodents that have evolved to be able to thrive in extreme conditions. The main environmental issues they face are mining, and the overuse of artesian water.

The Island of New Guinea

The island of New Guinea is rich in rainforest jungles, with a range of wildlife, much of which has not yet been studied by scientists. Mining in the past has resulted in environmental pollution which not only affected wildlife, but which also damaged the natural resources needed by the local people.

Beautiful Places

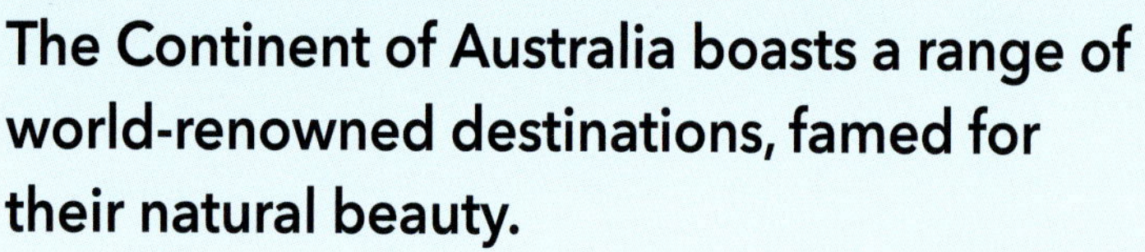

The Continent of Australia boasts a range of world-renowned destinations, famed for their natural beauty.

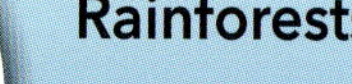

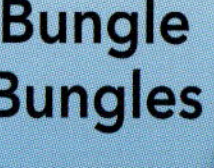

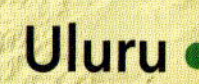

Glossary

abruptly very suddenly

artesian water water supply from natural underground reservoirs

continental shelf edges of a continent that extend outwards underwater

dingo native dog

dormant volcano volcano that is not erupting but may erupt in the future

missionary person who works to convert others to a different religion

monsoon seasonal change in wind direction, bringing either wet or dry seasons in tropical regions

nautical mile measurement of distance over water or when travelling in the air. It equals 1.85 kilometres

ocean abyss very deep part of an ocean

plate tectonics movement of large blocks of land across the Earth

spirit house religious place in a New Guinea village

subsistence farming producing only enough for one's own needs

urbanised living in cities

Dingoes are Australia's own native dogs

Spirit houses are traditional religious places found in New Guinea villages

Great Barrier Reef

Index

Marsupials p:24, 25, 29

Tarvurvur volcano